FRANK MILLER

DARK HORSE
MAVERICK

Mike Richardson • publisher

Randy Stradley • editor

Mark Cox & Brian Gogolin • collection design

Steve Miller • logo design

SIN CITY®

This volume collects stories originally appearing in issues
fifty-one through sixty-two of the Dark Horse comic-book series *Dark Horse Presents* and in
the Dark Horse comic book *Dark Horse Presents Fifth Anniversary Special*.

Published by Dark Horse Comics, Inc.
10956 S.E. Main Street
Milwaukie, OR 97222

www.darkhorse.com

To find a comics shop in your area,
call the Comic Shop Locator Service toll-free at 1-888-266-4226

First edition: January 1993
ISBN: 1-878574-59-0

10 9

Printed in Canada

THREE HOURS LATER I'VE GOT MY PANTS PULLED ON AND MY BOOTS LACED UP AND MY HEAD'S FEELING SEVERAL SIZES TOO BIG AND THAT COLD THING HAPPENS TO MY STOMACH AND I REALIZE THAT GOLDIE IS DEAD.

NOT A MARK ON HER. YOU'D HAVE TO CHECK HER PULSE OR NOTICE THOSE PERFECT BREASTS OF HERS AREN'T MOVING LIKE THEY WOULD IF SHE WAS BREATHING.

AND THERE'S NOTHING TELLING ME IT WASN'T JUST A HEART ATTACK IN HER SLEEP...

...NOTHING BUT THAT COLD THING IN MY GUT GETTING COLDER...

WHOEVER KILLED YOU IS GOING TO PAY, GOLDIE...

FUMPP

HNF?

CLAIRE?

MOM STILL HASN'T CHANGED A THING IN THIS ROOM. EVERY WEEK SHE DUSTS IT ALL OFF SO IT LOOKS LIKE IT WAS ONLY YESTERDAY I MOVED OUT.

AND EVERY TIME I COME VISIT SHE HAS ME SLEEP IN HERE AND THE OLD SMELLS MAKE ME CRY LIKE THEY DO RIGHT NOW.

I KNEW GLADYS WOULD BE SAFE HERE.

I WAS ALWAYS GOOD AT JIGSAW PUZZLES.

BACK IN SCHOOL I HAD THIS BUDDY, NAME OF CHUCK. HE WAS RETARDED. HE'D WATCH ME PUT THE PIECES TOGETHER AND I LOVED THAT GUY BECAUSE HE WAS THE ONLY PERSON I EVER MET WHO WAS DUMB ENOUGH TO THINK I WAS A GENIUS.

AND THE SITUATION I GOT RIGHT NOW, IT'S JUST ONE MORE JIGSAW PUZZLE. PROBLEM IS I'M DAMN SHORT ON PIECES.

I'VE BEEN FRAMED FOR MURDER AND THE COPS ARE IN ON IT. BUT THE REAL ENEMY, THE SON OF A BITCH WHO KILLED THE ANGEL LYING NEXT TO ME, HE'S OUT THERE SOMEWHERE, OUT OF SIGHT, THE BIG MISSING PIECE THAT'LL GIVE ME THE HOW AND THE WHY AND A FACE AND A NAME AND A SOUL TO SEND SCREAMING INTO HELL.

THE GOOD NEWS IS THAT THE KILLER ISN'T SITTING BACK AND WAITING FOR THE COPS TO POLISH ME OFF. *"THERE WERE SOME MEN WHO CAME LOOKING FOR YOU,"* MOM SAID, *"THEY WEREN'T POLICE."*

SO ALL I GOT TO DO IS SEND THE BASTARD AN INVITATION. HE'LL COME OR HE'LL SEND SOMEBODY AND EITHER WAY IF I DON'T GET DEAD I'M BOUND TO WIND UP WITH ONE OR TWO MORE PUZZLE PIECES.

TELL KADIE IT'S MARV. IT'LL BE OKAY.

OKAY.

HE'S NEW HERE, MARV. HE DIDN'T KNOW.

IN THIS TOWN JUST ABOUT ANYTHING YOU CAN NAME THAT'S WORTH DOING IS AGAINST THE LAW. IT WORKS OUT BETTER FOR EVERYBODY THIS WAY. COPS AND POLITICIANS MAKE THEIR FORTUNES BY LOOKING THE OTHER WAY WHILE CROOKS LIKE KADIE GET AWAY WITH CHARGING TEN BUCKS A DRINK.

BUT HERE AT KADIE'S MY DRINKS ARE ALWAYS FREE. THE SWEET OLD TRANSSEXUAL WOULD BREAK MY ARM IF I TRIED TO PAY. I'VE DONE HER FAVORS AND THERE'S NOBODY WHO KNOWS WHERE THE BODIES ARE BURIED.

NOBODY BUT ME.

KADIE'S IS MY KIND OF JOINT. COUNTRY, AND I DON'T MEAN THAT TOUCHY-FEELY *"YOU PUT ME ON A NATURAL HIGH"* GARBAGE THEY'RE PASSING OFF AS COUNTRY THESE DAYS. NO, AT KADIE'S IT'S THE OLD STUFF. IT'S CONWAY AND TAMMY AND MERLE, FROM BACK BEFORE THEY WENT ALL SQUISHY. SONGS TO DRINK TO AND TO CRY TO.

I'M HIT SQUARE IN THE CHEST WITH THE PLUMPED-UP-ALL-THE-WAY BASS OF EMMYLOU BELTING OUT *"DRIVING WHEEL"*.

MUST BE NANCY UP ON STAGE.

THAT'S HER FAVORITE SONG TO SHAKE IT TO.

...DIDN'T MEAN IT LORD I DIDN'T MEAN IT I DON'T KNOW WHAT GOT INTO ME YOU KNOW I LOVE YOU DARLING...

SIN CITY FALLS AWAY BEHIND ME, NOISY AND UGLY AS ALL HELL. THE MERCEDES HUMS AND HANDLES LIKE A DREAM. SHE MAY LOOK LIKE SOME JAP DESIGNED HER, BUT THE ENGINE'S A BEAUTY.

MY HEAD STARTS TO CLEAR. THINGS START TO MAKE SENSE.

THAT WASN'T GOLDIE BACK THERE. I LET MYSELF GET CONFUSED AGAIN. IT'S OKAY WHEN I SMELL THINGS THAT AREN'T THERE OR EVEN WHEN I HEAR THINGS. BUT IT'S PRETTY SERIOUS WHEN I SEE THINGS.

IT'S MY OWN FAULT AND NOBODY ELSE'S THAT I GOT CONFUSED. I WOULD'VE BEEN ALL RIGHT IF I TOOK MY MEDICINE WHEN I SHOULD HAVE.

I'VE BEEN HAVING SO MUCH FUN I FORGOT TO TAKE MY MEDICINE.

THAT WASN'T GOLDIE BACK THERE. GOLDIE IS DEAD AND THAT'S THE WHOLE REASON I'VE BEEN DOING WHAT I'VE BEEN DOING.

I FORGOT TO TAKE MY MEDICINE.

WHEN *YOU'VE* GOT A CONDITION IT'S BAD TO FORGET YOUR MEDICINE.

GULP

TWO MILES FROM
THE FARM I SPOT A
DINER AND LEAVE THE
MERCEDES IN THE
PARKING LOT AND MOVE
AHEAD ON FOOT. IF
THERE'S ANYTHING TO
WHAT THE PADRE TOLD
ME I'VE GOT TO PLAY
THIS CAREFUL.

EVEN IF IT MEANS
CUTTING THROUGH THE
WOODS AT NIGHT.

I HATE THE WOODS AT
NIGHT. ESPECIALLY THE
SOUNDS. PEOPLE ARE
ALWAYS TALKING ABOUT
NATURE LIKE IT'S ALL
SWEET AND FRIENDLY.
ALL I CAN FIGURE IS
THEY NEVER SPENT A
NIGHT TIED TO A TREE
IN THE WOODS.

EVER SINCE CAMP I'VE
HATED THE WOODS.

THERE ISN'T MUCH ELSE
THAT SCARES ME.

FOR A WHILE IT'S OUTER SPACE WITH NO STARS IN IT, COLD AND BLACK AND BOTTOMLESS. I TUMBLE, WEIGHTLESS AS A GHOST.

FOR A WHILE I'VE GOT NO BRAIN AND NO BODY AND THAT'S FINE BY ME.

THEN THE BROKEN BITS START WITH THEIR NAGGING. THE JAGGED LITTLE BASTARDS DANCE LIKE LEPRECHAUNS, PULLING TOGETHER IN A BULLIES' CIRCLE, LAUGHING AT ME, TELLING ME I'M AN EVEN BIGGER LOSER THAN I EVER THOUGHT I WAS.

THEY PLAY IT BACK FOR ME LIKE A MOVIE ON REWIND-- FROM THE SUNBURST OF THE SLEDGEHAMMER · HITTING MY FACE--BACK TO THE SOFT CHILLY SKIN OF THE GODDESS WHO WAS MURDERED IN MY BED.

I BLEW IT, GOLDIE. I FOUND YOUR KILLER BUT HE WAS BETTER THAN ME, TOO QUIET AND TOO QUICK, A KILLER BORN. HE TOOK ME OUT LIKE I WAS A GIRL SCOUT. HE DIDN'T EVEN BREAK A SWEAT...

...BUT IF I'M DOING ALL THIS THINKING, THAT MEANS I'M STILL ALIVE, DOESN'T IT?

WHY DIDN'T HE FINISH THE JOB?...OR IS THIS THE HELL I'VE SPENT MY WHOLE LIFE EARNING, FALLING, FOREVER FALLING, NEVER KNOWING?

THEN THE HURT COMES. THE LIVING HURT. STREAKING FROM BEHIND MY EYES. FINDING PLACES TO HAVE ITS FUN.

A SMELL HITS MY NOSTRILS, HARD, BURNING, ANTISEPTIC.

LIGHT GROWS.

I DIVE FOR IT.

DAMES, SOMETIMES ALL THEY GOT TO DO IS LET IT OUT AND A FEW BUCKETS LATER THERE'S NO WAY YOU'D EVER KNOW.

I WATCH LUCILLE SLIDE EVERY GORGEOUS INCH OF HERSELF INTO MY COAT. I SHAKE MY HEAD FOR WHAT MUST BE THE MILLIONTH TIME. HARDWARE LIKE SHE'S GOT AND LUCILLE'S A DYKE. IT'S A DAMN CRIME.

BUT I DON'T SAY A WORD ABOUT THAT. I PIPED UP AT HER ONCE THAT MAYBE SHE OUGHT TO GET TREATMENT OR SOMETHING AND SHE HAULED OFF AND NAILED ME WITH A PUNCH THAT SHOWED ME THERE WAS PLENTY OF MUSCLE UNDER ALL THAT HEAVEN.

BUT THAT WAS YEARS AGO AND IT HASN'T GOT ANYTHING TO DO WITH GETTING OUT OF HERE.

YOU'VE BROUGHT US SOME BIG TROUBLE THIS TIME, MARV. WHOEVER'S BEHIND ALL THIS HAS GOT HIS CONNECTIONS-- RIGHT IN THE DEPARTMENT. ANY LEADS?

NUFF

YEAH, I DID SOME NOSING AROUND.

ONE GUY I TALKED TO, HE TOLD ME IT WAS ROARK RUNNING THE SHOW.

THAT'S GOT TO BE BULLSHIT.

JUST TELLING YOU WHAT I BEEN TOLD.

WHUFF

WELL, WHOEVER IT IS, HE KNEW I WAS CHECKING OUT THAT HOOKER ALMOST BEFORE I DID.

WHAT HOOKER?

THE ONE YOU'VE BEEN OBSESSING OVER... THE DEAD ONE.

GOLDIE.

RAIN DOESN'T COME TO SIN CITY REAL OFTEN. AND WHEN IT DOES, IT'S USUALLY PRETTY LAME STUFF. WARM AS SWEAT AND LUCKY IF IT GETS TO THE PAVEMENT BEFORE IT EVAPORATES.

BUT MAYBE TWICE A YEAR, THE DESERT SKY REALLY COUGHS IT UP AND SPITS IT OUT. A COLD, MEAN TORRENT THAT TURNS THE STREETS TO GLASS AND CHILLS YOU TO THE BONE.

MOST PEOPLE HATE THE RAIN WHEN IT'S NASTY LIKE THIS. BUT ME, I LOVE IT. IT HELPS ME THINK.

I'M NOT REAL SMART, BUT I FEEL A WHOLE LOT SMARTER WHEN EVERYTHING GOES SLICK AND EVERYBODY SKITTERS OFF THE STREETS AND GETS OUT OF MY WAY.

I LOVE THE RAIN. I LOVE THE ICY WAY IT CREEPS DOWN MY NECK. THE WAY THE AIR GOES ELECTRIC AND EVERYTHING SEEMS SO CLEAR.

YOU BREATHE IN AND YOUR NOSTRILS WORK.

THAT'S WHAT I DO. I BREATHE IN AND I JUST LET MY FEET TAKE ME WHEREVER THEY WANT.

AND I THINK.

MY EYES STILL
WATCH OUT FOR A
SQUAD CAR OR A BEAT
COP BUT MY BRAIN
GOES OFF ON ITS
OWN, DEEP INSIDE,
SPREADING OUT THE
PUZZLE PIECES ONE
MORE TIME, TRYING
TO FIND TWO THAT'LL
FIT TOGETHER,
LOOKING FOR SOME
HINT OF THE BIG
PICTURE.

BUT MOSTLY I KEEP
COMING BACK TO
THAT COP I JUST
KILLED AND WHAT HE
TOLD ME.

HE WAS A TOUGH
ONE AND I WAS
PRETTY STEAMED
ABOUT WHAT HE
DONE TO LUCILLE
ANYWAY SO I TOOK
MY TIME WITH THE
SON OF A BITCH. IT
WASN'T UNTIL I
SHOWED HIM ALL
THOSE PIECES OF
HIMSELF THAT HE
SAID WHAT HE SAID.
THEN ALL OF A
SUDDEN HE WAS THE
ONE DOING THE
LAUGHING BECAUSE
HE SAW THE LOOK
ON MY FACE AND HE
DIED KNOWING I
WISHED TO GOD HE'D
KEPT HIS MOUTH
SHUT AFTER ALL.

IT WAS JUST A
NAME BUT I
HAVEN'T STOPPED
SHAKING SINCE I
HEARD IT. AND THE
RAIN ISN'T THE
REASON I'M
SHAKING, EITHER.

JUST A NAME. BACK
WHEN THE PREIST
SAID IT I FIGURED HE
WAS JERKING MY
CHAIN. BUT HEARING IT
FROM THE COP I KNEW
IT COULDN'T BE A
COINCIDENCE.

JUST A NAME.

ROARK.

ROARK!

DAMN IT!

EVERY INCH OF ME WANTS TO TURN TAIL. TO SNEAK INTO THE BACK OF A TRUCK OR HOP A FREIGHT CAR AND HAUL OUT OF TOWN. I WANT TO RUN, RUN LIKE HELL, TO CRAWL INTO A CAVE SOMEWHERE AND FORGET ABOUT GOLDIE AND LUCILLE AND SILENT, DEADLY KEVIN.

ROARK. DAMN IT.

I'M AS GOOD AS DEAD.

I'M AS GOOD AS DEAD.

AND IT'S NOT THAT I'M ANY KIND OF HERO THAT MAKES ME STAY. HEROES DON'T GO WEAK IN THE KNEES AND FEEL LIKE THROWING UP OR CURLING UP INTO A LITTLE BALL AND CRYING LIKE A BABY.

AND EVEN THOUGH MY LIFE WOULD BE NOTHING BUT AN ENDLESS GREY HELL OF BOOZE AND BRAWLS LIKE IT WAS BEFORE, I'M MORE SCARED OF DYING THAN I AM OF LIVING.

NO, I'M NO HERO. NOT BY A LONG SHOT. I JUST KNOW GOLDIE WON'T LET ME OFF SO EASY. NO MATTER WHERE I GO I'LL SMELL HER ANGEL SMELL. I'LL SEE THAT MOUTH AND THOSE EYES AND THAT PERFECT, PERFECT BODY. I'LL HEAR HER AND I'LL TASTE HER AND I'LL KNOW IT WAS ME, ONLY ME, WHO COULD HAVE SET THINGS RIGHT.

YOU WERE SCARED, WEREN'T YOU, GOLDIE? SOMEBODY WANTED YOU DEAD AND YOU KNEW IT. SO YOU HIT THE SALOONS, THE BAD PLACES, LOOKING FOR THE BIGGEST, MEANEST LUG AROUND AND FINDING ME.

LOOKING FOR PROTECTION AND PAYING FOR IT WITH YOUR BODY AND MORE --WITH LOVE, WITH WILD FIRE, MAKING ME FEEL LIKE A KING, LIKE A DAMN WHITE KNIGHT.

LIKE A HERO.

WHAT A LAUGH.

YOU WANTED ME TO KEEP YOU SAFE BUT WHEN THAT BASTARD CAME TO KILL YOU I WAS STONE DRUNK.

BLACKED OUT.

USELESS.

"SAINT PATRICK," THEY CALL HIM BUT IT'S JUST A NICKNAME. THE POPE HASN'T GOTTEN AROUND TO MAKING IT OFFICIAL. NOT YET, ANYWAY.

THE ROARK FAMILY HAS OWNED SIN CITY SINCE THE DAYS OF WAGON TRAINS AND SIXGUNS. OVER THE GENERATIONS THEIR MILLIONS HAVE GROWN TO BILLIONS. THEY'RE KIND OF LIKE OUR OWN ROYAL FAMILY.

THIS PARTICULAR GENERATION PRODUCED A UNITED STATES SENATOR, A STATE ATTORNEY GENERAL--AND PATRICK HENRY ROARK.

CARDINAL ROARK.

BACK IN SCHOOL THE SISTERS WOULD NEVER SHUT UP ABOUT HIM. MAN OF THE CLOTH. WAR HERO IN THE MEDICAL CORPS. PHILANTHROPIST. EDUCATOR. COULD'VE BECOME PRESIDENT BUT HE CHOSE TO SERVE GOD.

AND ALONG THE WAY HE JUST HAPPENED TO BECOME THE MOST POWERFUL MAN IN THE STATE. HE'S BROUGHT DOWN MAYORS AND GOTTEN GOVERNORS ELECTED.

AND HERE HE'S GOING TO GET KILLED IN THE NAME OF A DEAD HOOKER.

I'M GETTING USED TO THE IDEA.

MORE AND MORE I'M LIKING THE SOUND OF IT.

THE RAIN'S SPUTTERED TO A STOP AND THE STREETS HAVE COME BACK TO LIFE BY THE TIME I MAKE MY WAY TO OLD TOWN.

THE MERCHANDISE IS ON DISPLAY, NEVER MIND THE COLD. PRETTY SOON EVERYTHING FROM PICKUPS TO LIMOS WILL BE PULLING IN AND BUSINESS WILL BE BOOMING.

OLD TOWN IS WHY NOBODY CALLS THIS BURG "BASIN CITY" LIKE IT SAYS ON THE MAPS.

IT WAS SAINT PATRICK'S GREAT GRANDFATHER WHO MADE IT HAPPEN. BACK THEN THIS WAS A GOLD RUSH TOWN ON ITS WAY TO BECOMING A GHOST TOWN.

THEN OLD MAN ROARK GOT HIMSELF AN IDEA.

HE SPENT EVERY SILVER DOLLAR HE HAD, IMPORTING TOP HOOKERS FROM FRANCE AND PLACES LIKE THAT.

WORD GOT OUT AND PRETTY SOON SIN CITY WAS THE HOTTEST STOP IN THE WEST. PEOPLE WOULD COME FROM MILES AROUND.

THEY STILL DO AND IT'S EASY TO SEE WHY. OLD TOWN'S KEPT ITS TRADITIONS, HANDED DOWN FROM GORGEOUS MOTHER TO GORGEOUS DAUGHTER.

FOR AN HOUR OR SO I ASK AROUND ABOUT GOLDIE. I DON'T GET ANY ANSWERS BUT I KNOW I'M BOUND TO. LUCILLE SAID GOLDIE WAS A HOOKER AND IF SHE WAS SHE HAS ROOTS HERE. FRIENDS.

MAYBE EVEN FAMILY.

I WIPE THE BLOOD OFF AND I TAKE A DEEP BREATH AND I TAKE A GOOD LONG LOOK AT THE MONSTER IN THE MIRROR.

DON'T SCREW UP THIS TIME, MARV. IT'S TOO IMPORTANT. RIGHT NOW, WHILE YOU'RE ALONE, FEEL THE FEAR AND GET PAST IT. GO AHEAD. SHAKE LIKE A JUNKIE. LET YOUR HEART CRAWL UP YOUR THROAT. LET YOUR STOMACH SQUEEZE ITSELF INTO A GOLF BALL, INTO ONE OF THOSE BLACK HOLES THAT SUCKS EVERYTHING INTO IT.

THINK ABOUT DYING. THINK HARD. PICTURE IT. A BULLET THROUGH YOUR BRAIN AND THAT'S IF YOU'RE LUCKY, GETTING IT THAT QUICK.

BUT IT'S JUST AS LIKELY GOING TO BE THE SLOW WAY. A LONG, BAD JOKE OF A TRIAL AND A LONGER WAIT IN A CELL UNTIL THEY STRAP YOU INTO THAT CHAIR AND A MILLION VOLTS SEND YOU STRAIGHT TO HELL AND THEY'LL CALL YOU A PSYCHO KILLER WHO GOT WHAT WAS COMING TO HIM.

PICTURE IT. FEEL IT. GET USED TO IT. THEN PUT IT BACK INSIDE WHERE IT BELONGS. YOU'VE GOT SOME PEOPLE TO KILL. AND IF YOU DO IT RIGHT IT WON'T MATTER WHAT ANYBODY SAYS. YOU'LL GO TO YOUR GRAVE A WINNER.

I TRY NOT TO LOOK AT HER TOO MUCH. IT MAKES IT WORSE WHEN I DO. BUT WHEN I CLOSE MY EYES FOR TOO LONG IT HAPPENS ANYWAY. I GET CONFUSED AND START THINKING SHE'S GOLDIE. SHE'S GOT THE SMELL AND THE VOICE JUST LIKE SHE'S GOT THE LOOKS. EVERYTHING'S TELLING ME SHE'S GOLDIE AND I HAVE TO KEEP REMINDING MYSELF SHE ISN'T. GOLDIE'S DEAD AND THE ANGEL SITTING NEXT TO ME, SHE'S WENDY. GOLDIE'S TWIN SISTER.

AND SHE'S ONE TOUGH BIRD. SHE'S BOUNCED ME AROUND A PARKING LOT WITH HER CUTE LITTLE PORSCHE. SHE'S SHOT ME AND PISTOL WHIPPED ME AND IT TOOK SOME FAST TALKING TO KEEP HER FROM BLOWING MY BRAINS OUT.

SHE'S WENDY. GOLDIE'S TWIN SISTER.

I CAN'T LET MYSELF GET CONFUSED ABOUT THAT.

IT WAS A FARM BOY NAME OF KEVIN WHO KILLED GOLDIE. NEVER SEEN ANYTHING LIKE HIM. KNOCKED ME FLAT. BUT IT'S ROARK WHO'S BEHIND IT AND I DON'T KNOW WHY. CARDINAL ROARK.

ROARK. NO KIDDING.

"GOLDIE WORKED THE CLERGY"... JUST LIKE THAT A WHOPPER OF A PUZZLE PIECE FALLS SMACK IN MY LAP. I'M TOO DUMB TO PUT THE WHOLE PICTURE TOGETHER YET, BUT...

...BUT SHE FIRES UP TWO CIGARETTES AND HANDS ME ONE AND I TASTE HER LIPSTICK ON IT AND SUDDENLY MY HEART'S POUNDING SO LOUD I CAN'T HEAR ANYTHING ELSE. I WANT TO CRY AND I WANT TO LAUGH AT THE CRAZINESS OF IT ALL BUT MOSTLY I WANT TO REACH OVER AND TOUCH HER AND TASTE GOLDIE'S SWEAT ONE MORE TIME.

BUT SHE ISN'T GOLDIE.

THE SUN GOES DOWN GOOD AND EARLY SO THE STORES ARE STILL OPEN. WENDY AND ME GO SHOPPING WITH HER MONEY.

YEAH. THIS'LL DO. I'M ALSO GONNA BE NEEDING A DOZEN TWO-FOOT LENGTHS OF RUBBER TUBING AND A SPOOL OF RAZOR WIRE AND THOSE SPECIAL GLOVES THAT'LL LET ME HANDLE THE WIRE.

BEEFING UP THE OLD HOME SECURITY, HUH?

YOU SHOULDN'T OUGHT TO POKE YOUR NOSE INTO PEOPLE'S PRIVATE BUSINESS.

STOP AT THE NEXT GAS STATION.

BUT THE TANK'S FULL...

...OH. NEVER MIND.

HER EYES ARE BURNING HOLES THROUGH ME BUT STILL SHE DOESN'T ASK. SHE KNOWS I'M THE ONLY CHANCE SHE HAS.

STAY HERE. KEEP THE ENGINE RUNNING. IF I'M NOT BACK IN TWENTY MINUTES, GET THE HELL OUT OF HERE AND DON'T LOOK BACK.

KILL HIM FOR ME, MARV. KILL HIM GOOD.

I WON'T LET YOU DOWN, GOLDIE. I PROMISED.

IT ISN'T LONG
BEFORE I BREAK
INTO A RUN. I CAN'T
HELP MYSELF.

NO SHAKING, NOW.
NO COLD SWEAT. NO
DOUBTS. THE FEAR
GOT OUT FOR A
LITTLE WHILE THERE
BUT NOW IT'S
CRAWLED BACK IN,
FAR AWAY, A SMALL
COLD THING LOST
IN A BELLY THAT'S
FULL OF FIRE.

EVEN THE WOODS
DON'T SCARE ME
ANYMORE BECAUSE
I'M JUST ONE MORE
PREDATOR AND I'M
BIGGER AND
MEANER THAN
THE REST.

ALL I'VE EVER
BEEN GOOD AT IS
KILLING SO I
MIGHT AS WELL
ENJOY IT.

FOR A WHILE I JUST TRY TO
SLOW MY HEART DOWN AND BREATHE
THE FIRE OUT OF MY LUNGS. MY
MUSCLES MAKE ME A THOUSAND
PROMISES OF PAIN TO COME. IT'LL
BE A ROUGH MORNING IF I'M
ALIVE TO SEE IT.

THE NIGHT'S ALL
WEIRD AND QUIET.
SO QUIET THE
CRICKETS SEEM
LOUD.

KEFF

THEN THERE'S A
GENTLE FLAP OF
FABRIC AND LIGHT
FOOTSTEPS ON THE
GRASS.

AND THAT
SCENT.

...NOT EVEN AT THE END.

NOT EVEN WHEN THE MUTT'S HAD HIS FILL AND KEVIN'S GUTS ARE LYING ALL OVER THE PLACE AND SOMEHOW THE BASTARD IS STILL ALIVE, STILL STARING AT ME.

NOT EVEN WHEN I GRAB THE SAW AND FINISH THE JOB.

HE NEVER SCREAMS!

THE *MISSION.*

"*FORTRESS ROARK*" IS **WHAT** SOME PEOPLE CALL IT AND IF YOU ASK ME THEY AREN'T WRONG. ROARK'S **BEEN** HOLED UP THERE FOR YEARS, SURROUNDED BY A SQUAD OF ARMED GUARDS, SITTING PRETTY WHILE MAYORS AND SENATORS AND GOVERNORS COME, HATS IN HAND, BEGGING FAVORS FROM MIGHTY SAINT PATRICK.

I'D LIKE TO BLOW THE WHOLE DAMNED PLACE SKY HIGH. TO WIPE IT OUT AND LEAVE A CRATER BIG ENOUGH AND DEEP ENOUGH TO SUCK IN ALL THE MONEY AND LIES OF ALL THE GENERATIONS OF THE ROYAL ROARK FAMILY.

BUT THAT'S JUST ENTHUSIASM TALKING. I'VE GOT TO PLAY THIS SNEAKY. SNEAKY AND VERY, VERY NASTY.

THIS IS IT, GOLDIE. WIN OR LOSE, IT'S ALL OVER TONIGHT.

JERKS! THEY SHOULD HAVE SHOT ME IN THE HEAD--AND ENOUGH TIMES TO MAKE SURE.

A FEW DAYS LATER I CLAW MY WAY OUT OF A HAZE OF ANESTHETICS. IT'S UP TO THE DOCTORS FOR NOW, THE DOCTORS AND THE REAL HARD WORKERS, THE NURSES.

IT'S STUPID. EVERYBODY KNOWS WHAT'S COMING BUT THEY GO THROUGH THE MOTIONS ANYWAY. WHAT A WASTE OF TIME.

MONTHS FALL OFF THE CALENDAR WHILE I BREATHE AND EAT THROUGH TUBES AND I CAN'T EVEN WASH MYSELF OR USE A TOILET LIKE A GROWN MAN OUGHT TO.

NIGHT AFTER NIGHT I WAIT FOR SOMEBODY TO COME AND FINISH ME OFF. AFTER AWHILE I REALIZE IT'S NOT GOING TO BE SO EASY AS THAT. I'M A MONKEY WRENCH STUCK IN A GREAT BIG MACHINE AND I'VE CAUSED SOME DAMAGE AND IT'LL TAKE A GOOD LONG TIME FOR THE GEARS TO GRIND ME TO POWDER.

I'M ON MY FEET FOR ABOUT TEN MINUTES BEFORE THE COPS KICK THEM OUT FROM UNDER ME. THEY DON'T ASK ME ANY QUESTIONS. THEY JUST KEEP KNOCKING THE CRAP OUT OF ME AND WAVING A CONFESSION IN MY FACE.

AND I KEEP SPITTING BLOOD ALL OVER IT AND LAUGHING AT HOW MANY FRESH COPIES THEY COME UP WITH.

MOSTLY I DON'T FEEL THE PUNISHMENT. I'M OFF, FAR AWAY, WATCHING IT ALL GO PAST LIKE AN OLD MOVIE YOU ALREADY KNOW THE END OF.

THEN ALONG COMES THIS WORMY ASSISTANT DISTRICT ATTORNEY WHO TURNS THE RECORDER OFF AND SAYS IF I DON'T SIGN THEIR CONFESSION THEY'LL KILL MY MOM.

I BREAK HIS ARM IN THREE PLACES AND SIGN THE CONFESSION.

FROM THEN ON IT'S THE CIRCUS EVERYBODY WANTS IT TO BE. THEY NAIL ME FOR THE WORKS. NOT JUST THE PEOPLE I DID KILL BUT EVEN LUCILLE AND THE GIRLS ROARK AND KEVIN ATE.

AND EVEN GOLDIE.

THE JUDGE IS ALL FIRE AND BRIMSTONE WHEN SHE HANDS DOWN THE SENTENCE. THE CROWD EATS IT UP.

AND RIGHT NOW THEY'RE OUTSIDE, WAITING, HOLDING A VIGIL, THEY CALL IT. THEY'RE HOLLERING AND PULLING SIX PACKS OUT OF THEIR STATION WAGONS AND WISHING THEY COULD WATCH THE LYNCHING UP CLOSE. THEY'LL HAVE TO SETTLE FOR WATCHING THE LIGHTS DIM.

MIDNIGHT AND MY DEATH ARE ONLY A FEW HOURS AWAY WHEN I GET MY FIRST SURPRISE IN EIGHTEEN MONTHS.

MY ONLY VISITOR.

THEY'VE GOT ME IN A CELL ABOUT A MILE AWAY FROM THE OTHER CONS SO I CAN HEAR HER HEELS CLICK ON THE CEMENT FLOOR FOR A LONG TIME BEFORE SHE GETS HERE.

I'M READY FOR ANYTHING BUT THAT SCENT.

I GOT THEM FOR YOU GOOD, DIDN'T I, GOLDIE?

THIS ONE'S FOR LYNN

his one ran away with itself. I'd planned it as forty-eight pages, but I got carried away. It's all Marv's fault. The big lug started bossing me around. It's like that sometimes. The pages you're looking at right now feature some of the covers and publicity pieces I drew in the course of Sin City's thirteen month run in Dark Horse Presents, the monthly anthology comic.

Sin City is the first of a projected series of graphic stories that I can't wait to get drawing. I hope you've gotten a kick out of this one.

FM

OTHER YARNS FROM SIN CITY